The Sky between homes

By **Emily Drage**

This is a work of fiction. Names, characters, places, and incidents are products of the author's imagination or are used fictitiously. Any resemblance to actual events, locales, or persons, living or dead, is purely coincidental.

Dedication

To all my wonderful foster children,
Who have grown to be amazing humans.

Your courage, your kindness, and your resilience inspire me every
day.

This story is for you!

Table of Contents

Author's Note

When I first sat down to write this story, I thought about all the incredible young people I've had the privilege to know—children who have lived through more pain, upheaval, and uncertainty than anyone ever should, yet who somehow still find a way to hope, to dream, and to keep going.

This book is for you.

I know foster care can feel lonely. I know it can feel like nobody really sees you, like nobody understands what it's like to pack your life into a bag over and over again and try to start fresh. I know how hard it is to let yourself trust, to let yourself believe that you deserve good things.

But you do.

You deserve safety. You deserve kindness. You deserve love. You deserve the chance to build a life that feels like your own. You deserve your quiet place!

I hope this story reminded you that you are not alone—and that your story is far from over. Every step you take, no matter how small, is worth celebrating.

To all my wonderful foster kids—past, present, and future—you inspire me every single day. You've grown into such amazing, strong, beautiful humans, and I am so proud of you.

With love,
Emily Drage

xoxo

Acknowledgements

This book was written for the kids who never felt like they had a place to belong. You are seen. You are valued. You are worthy of love.

To the countless young people who grow up in foster care, who carry more than their share of pain yet still dare to dream—your strength is breathtaking.

To the foster parents, social workers, and mentors who show up day after day: thank you for proving that kindness matters.

To my friends and family, who listened to every draft and cheered me on when I felt like giving up—your faith in me gave me wings.

And finally, to every reader who picks up this book and sees themselves in Skye's story: your best is yet to come!

Chapter 1: The seventeenth house

The first thing I notice is the silence.
No traffic. No shouting. No TV buzzing through the walls.
Just wind. And birds. And the creaking of an old screen door
that's probably haunted.

I stand at the edge of the gravel driveway, my duffel bag
heavy on my shoulder and my stomach knotted like barbed
wire. Megan and Will stand on the porch, smiling like this is
some kind of welcome home.

I don't smile back.

They wave, and Megan says, "Hi, Skye. We're really glad
you're here."

I nod because it feels easier than talking.

The house looks small but solid — a red tin roof, weathered
timber walls. Eucalyptus trees cast long shadows in the late
afternoon sun. The smell of damp earth and gum leaves fills
the air.

I remember the last place — cramped, noisy, strangers who never smiled. The foster homes blur together, like photos smudged by rain.
This is number seventeen.
I'm not sure if I'm ready to try again.

Megan gestures toward the porch steps. "Come on inside. We've got your room ready."

I take one step forward. Then another. The gravel crunches under my boots. My fingers tighten around the strap of my bag.

Inside, the house smells faintly of toast and lemon myrtle. The walls are painted soft cream, and a bunch of kids' drawings are pinned to the fridge — crooked smiles and stick figures holding hands.

"This is your room," Megan says, opening a door at the end of the hall.
It's small, but clean. A single bed with a blue quilt. A desk with a lamp. A window looking out to the paddock where a dark shape moves.

I set my bag down and peek out.
There, in the paddock, stands a horse. Black as midnight, muscles taut under a tangled mane. It watches me with sharp eyes.

Megan smiles. "That's Juno. She's a bit scared, but she's friendly once you get to know her."

I watch the horse for a moment longer, then close the window blinds.

The quiet feels like it's waiting. Waiting for me to break.

I lie on the bed and pull my sketchbook from my bag. It's worn — the cover soft from years of folding and unfolding. I open it to the first page, where a faded pencil drawing of a bird's wing curls on the paper.

I trace the lines with my finger.

Maybe here, I can learn how to fly again.

Chapter 2: The boy and the horse

The boy doesn't talk.

I first see him when I'm unpacking my things. He's sitting on the porch steps, arms wrapped around his knees, staring at the dirt road like it's the end of the world.

When I glance his way, he looks up and gives me one long look — like he's warning me not to get too close.
That's fine. I don't do talking either.

Later, I wander out to the paddock. Juno is there, pacing near the fence, nostrils flaring.

I hold out my hand, trying to be calm.
Juno snarls and snaps, teeth flashing.

"Don't worry," Megan calls from the porch. "She's just scared."

I watch the horse for a long time. There's something broken in her eyes, a wildness that makes my chest ache.
I get it.

The boy appears beside me.

"I'm Tom," he says, voice low.

"Skye," I answer.

He shrugs. "Don't expect much. I've been here a while."

We stand in silence, watching Juno shift restlessly.

"She bites," I say.

Tom smirks. "Yeah. That's Juno. She's been through stuff. Like us."

I nod slowly, feeling a strange bond forming.

Megan walks over with a bucket of feed.

"Maybe if you spend time with her, she'll start to trust you," she says kindly.

Tom rolls his eyes, but I think he means it.

That night, I lie in bed and sketch Juno's fierce eyes and tangled mane. I draw the wildness and the fear. The hurt.

Maybe some things need time to heal.

Chapter 3: The sky between us

At night, when the world is quiet and the stars come out like scattered diamonds, I climb onto the roof of the shed.

It's my secret place.

I lie back and open my sketchbook, drawing birds. Migratory birds. They never settle in one place too long. They keep moving, searching for a home that feels right.

I wonder if they're like me.

One night the neighbour Tahlia finds me the shed roof. She's also from school — bright, loud, and annoying in a good way.

"Hey," she says, sitting down beside me without asking.
I close my sketchbook quickly. "What do you want?"
"To be your friend," she says.
I laugh — a short, bitter sound. "I don't do friends."
"Sure you do," she says. "You just don't want to admit it."
We lie there under the sky, the air cool and soft.
"Why do you draw birds?" she asks.

"Because they fly away," I say. "Because they don't have to stay."

She's quiet for a moment.

"Maybe," she says finally, "sometimes you have to stay to find where you belong."

I look at her, really look, and something inside me shifts.

Maybe this house.
This foster family.
This strange new life — it isn't just another place to leave.

Maybe it's the sky between homes.

Chapter 4: Cracks in the fence

The morning sun filtered through the gum trees, casting dappled light on the paddock. I was already outside, sitting on the fence rail with my sketchbook balanced on my knee. Juno was grazing nearby, her black coat glistening in the early light.

Tom appeared from the farmhouse, boots crunching on the gravel. He didn't say hi. Instead, he walked straight over to the broken part of the fence—the one Juno had kicked the day before.

"She's a handful," he muttered, kneeling down to inspect the splintered wood. "This is the third time she's done that."
I didn't answer. Instead, I watched as Juno flicked her tail and stamped her hooves, restless and tense.
Tom straightened and glanced at me. "You're getting closer with her."
I shrugged. "Maybe. She's scared, like me."
He didn't laugh this time.

Megan came outside with a kettle and two mugs of tea.

"Breakfast in ten minutes," she called, then eyed the fence. "We'll have to fix that soon."

We sat in the kitchen later, the smell of toast and marmalade thick in the air. Megan and Will talked about their years fostering kids, the good days and the terrible ones. I realized they weren't just people who took us in— they carried their own scars.

Tom told me about his old foster home, the one he ran from, the reason he locked himself inside his shell.

"I don't trust people," he said quietly.
"Neither do I," I admitted.

But in the cracks of that old fence, I saw something fragile starting to grow—maybe trust.

Chapter 5: Storm clouds

That afternoon, dark clouds rolled over the hills like an angry sea. The wind picked up, rattling the windows and bending the branches of the gum trees.

Megan looked out the window, brow furrowed. "Looks like a storm's coming."

I sat with Tom and Tahlia at school, but my thoughts were elsewhere — on the storm, on the way my heart clenched every time I thought about leaving again.

Later that evening, the storm hit in full force. Thunder roared and rain pounded on the tin roof like a million drums.
I curled up in my bed, but sleep wouldn't come.

My phone buzzed—Megan's message. "Your caseworker's coming tomorrow."

Panic squeezed my chest. The caseworker. ...
The one who decides where I go next.
I wanted to run.

The next morning, I almost did. I grabbed my bag, planning to disappear down the dirt road.

Tom caught me at the gate. "Where do you think you're going?"
"Anywhere but here."
He didn't say anything. Just grabbed my hand and pulled me back.

Later, Juno bolted, terrified by the thunder. She crashed through the fence, disappearing into the bush.
We all scrambled after her—Megan, Will, Tom, me—calling her name into the pouring rain.
I felt my heart break with every step.

When we finally found Juno, trembling and tangled in brambles, something inside me cracked too.

I couldn't leave—not yet.

Chapter 6: Wings to fly

Weeks passed, and Juno slowly healed, just like me.
I spent more time with her, brushing her mane, whispering
stories I didn't say out loud.
Tom helped too, and slowly, our silence turned into
conversations.

At school, Tahlia pulled me into the art room. "You have to
enter the art contest," she said excitedly.
I laughed. "Why? So everyone can see how broken I am?"
She smiled. "Because your drawings are real. They tell
stories that need to be heard."

So I entered, painting a large canvas of a black-winged bird
soaring across a stormy sky. It was a story of loss, fear, and
hope all at once.

Foster family dinners became our tradition.

Megan made her famous damper bread, and we shared
stories and laughter, awkward but real.

One night, I stood outside, looking up at the stars. The birds I drew — they fly so far, searching for home.

Maybe I was one of them.

But maybe, just maybe, this was where I could finally rest.

Chapter 7: The nest we build

The school term was coming to an end, but the tension inside me felt heavier than ever.

Eighteen — that number echoed in my mind like a countdown.

Soon, I'd have to leave the foster system for good. No more homes, no more second chances.

Megan and Will sat me down one evening after dinner. Will's hands were rough from farm work, but his eyes were soft. "Skye," Megan said gently, "we know you're scared. But you're not alone. We want to help you figure out what comes next."

I swallowed hard, afraid to hope. "What if I fail? What if I'm just... broken?"

Will smiled. "No one's perfect. But you're stronger than you think."

For the first time, I felt a flicker of something — maybe hope, maybe trust.

Chapter 8: Wings unfolding

At school, the art contest was the talk of the town.
My painting of the black-winged bird stood tall in the hall,
drawing whispers and stares.

During the award ceremony, I felt my heart race as my name
was called.

I walked up to the stage, hands trembling.

"This is for everyone who feels lost but keeps flying," I said,
my voice barely steady.

The applause was louder than I expected. I looked into the
crowd and saw Tom smiling faintly, Tahlia cheering.

It wasn't just about winning. It was about being seen.

Chapter 9: Home is a flight

Spring arrived with blooming wildflowers and longer days.

Juno was healthy and calm now, no longer the wild horse she'd been.

One afternoon, Tom and I sat by the creek, skipping stones.
"I think... I'm ready to try," he said quietly.
"Try what?" I asked.
"Trust. Staying. Not running."
I smiled, feeling the weight lift from my shoulders.

Home wasn't a perfect place or a person.

It was a feeling — of safety, belonging, and the sky between us.

Chapter 10: The flight begins

The day I turned eighteen, the house was quiet in a way that felt both heavy and light.

Megan made pancakes for breakfast—my favourite—and Will handed me a small package wrapped in brown paper. Inside was a new sketchbook, blank and waiting.

"This is yours," Megan said softly. "For your next chapter."

I looked around the kitchen—the walls covered in photos and drawings, the smell of lemon myrtle still lingering.

I wasn't sure what the future held, but for the first time, I wasn't afraid.

Tom was there too, leaning against the doorframe, giving me a thumbs up.
"Ready to fly?" he asked.

I smiled, feeling something I hadn't felt in a long time: hope.
"Yes," I said. "I'm ready."

Epilogue: Between homes and sky

I stood at the edge of the paddock, sketchbook in hand, watching a flock of black cockatoos fly across the bright blue sky.

They moved as one, wings beating strong, calling to each other.

I thought about all the places I'd been—seventeen houses, countless faces—and the long road behind me.

But I also thought about the road ahead.

The homes I'd left were chapters in my story, but they didn't define me.

What mattered was the sky between homes—the space where I could grow, fall, and learn to fly on my own.

And as the cockatoos disappeared into the horizon, I whispered, "I'm ready."

Because sometimes, the hardest part isn't finding a home. It's learning to believe you deserve one.

www.ingramcontent.com/pod-product-compliance
Lightning Source LLC
Chambersburg PA
CBHW062105270326

41931CB00013B/3221